THE STORY OF SAINT CONSTANTINE

Biography for Kids

Children's Biography Books

BABY PROFESSOR

EDUCATION KIDS

Speedy Publishing LLC

40 E. Main St. #1156

Newark, DE 19711

www.speedypublishing.com

Copyright 2017

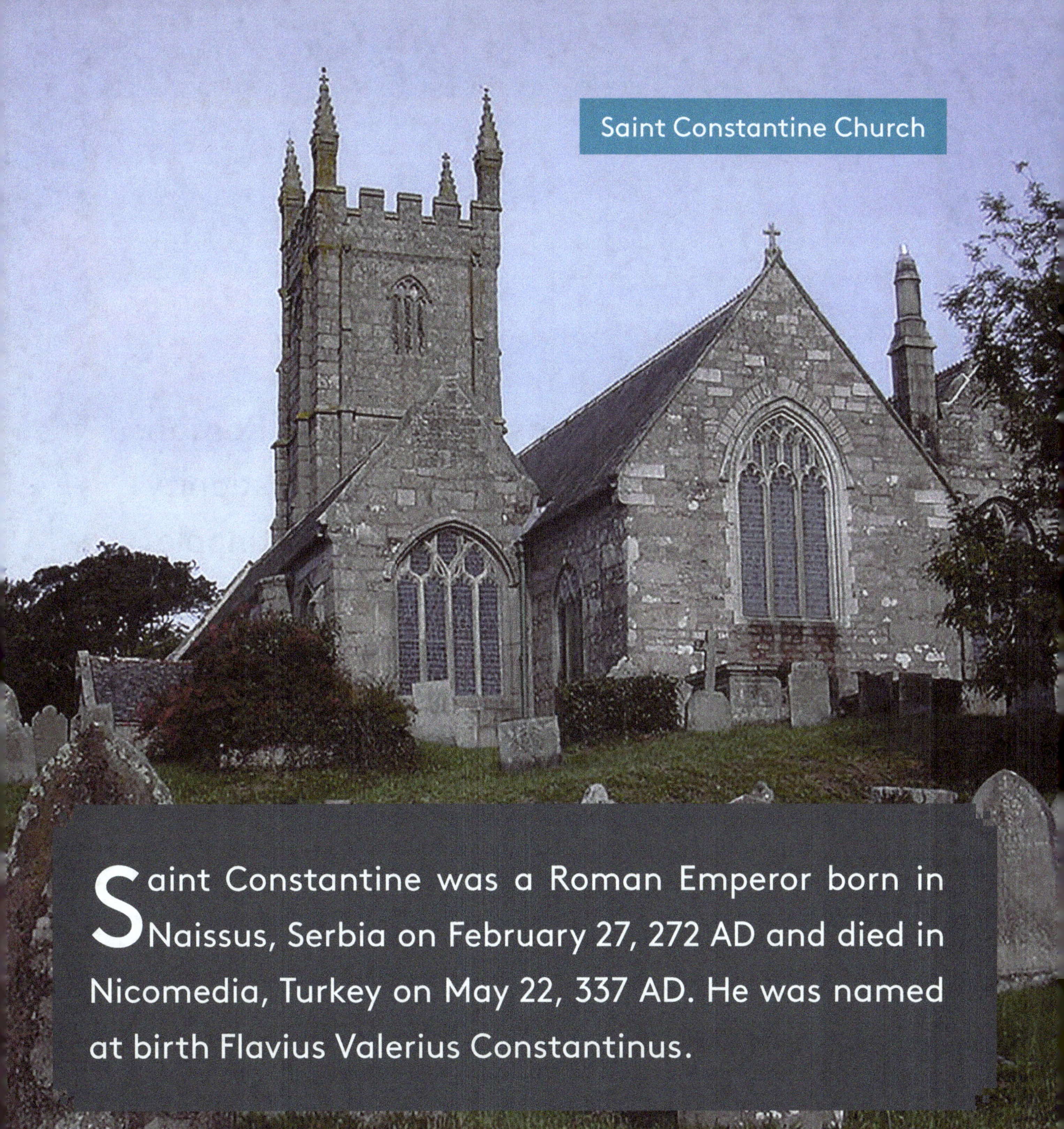

Saint Constantine was a Roman Emperor born in Naissus, Serbia on February 27, 272 AD and died in Nicomedia, Turkey on May 22, 337 AD. He was named at birth Flavius Valerius Constantinus.

He was known as the original Roman Emperor that converted to Christianity and established the city Of Constantinople. He is also referred to as Constantine the Great and Constantine I. Read further to learning more about his life and his death.

City of Constantinople

Roman Provinces

Acumincium
Argidava
Burridava
DACIA
SENS
Taurunum
Aquae
Herculis
Acumincium
Lederata
Pincum
Tierna
ALU
Viminacium
Cuppae
Novado
Pons Traiani
Rusidava
DACIA
Municipium
Taliata
Drobetae
Amutria
Tiasum
PIEPHIGIS
Idimum
Egeta
Acidava
Aquae
Dorticum
Pulonda
Pelendava
Romula
Horreum
Margi
Bononia
Almus
Potula
CIAGISII
Apiaria
Ratiaria
Augustae
Oescus
Sectorisca
Pista
Praes.Dasmini
Ciabrus
Novae
Trimammium
MOESIA
TRIBALLI
MOESIA
INFERIO
Praes. Pompei
Timacum
min.
Melta
Iatrum
SUPERIOR
Nicopolis
ad Istrum
CROY
Naissus
Remesiana
MOESIA
Tyle
Cabyle
DARDANIA
Turres
Meldia
Mons
Vindenis
Scupi
Scomius M.
Serdica (Ulpia)
CORALLI
Telanis
SERDI
Sub-
radice
Dereltu
Ulpiana
Bagaraca
Beroea
AGRIANES
Lissae
Sae
Pautalia
Bessapara
Hebrus
Tarp
Scardus M.
Dunax M.
DENTHE-
LETAE
BESSI
Philippopolis
(Trimontium)
Arsus
ODRY
AE
Axius
MAEDI
Rhodope M.
Bordipta
Hadrian
(Ores
Bylazora
Astibus
Strymon
Orbelus M.
Nicopolis
BENNI
PAEONIA
Doberus
SATRAE
COELETAE
THRACI
Stobi
SINTI
Plotinopolis
DEURIOPES
Prasias L.
ODOMANTI
Sirrhae
SAPAEI
TRAUSI
CORPILI
MACEDONIA
Philippi
PAET
Pelagonia
EDONES
Crenides
Abdera
CICONE
Trajanopolis
Cypsela
Heraclea
Lyncestis
Pangaeus
M.
Maronea
Doriscus
APSINTHII
Bora
M.
Pella
Amphipolis
Thasus
Aenos
L. Begor-
rius
Aegae
Sin. Strymonic.
SamoThrace
Callipolis
Edessa
Bermius
M.
Thessalonica
(Therma)
MARE THRACICUM
Sestus
Orestis
Beroea
CHALCIDICE
Imbros
Abydus
M. Elimea
Pydna
Olynthus
Sinus
Dium
Athos M.
Olympus

WHERE DID HE GROW UP?

He was born in Naissus approximately 272 AD. This city was located in the Roman province of Moesia, now known as Serbia. His father, Flavius Constantinus, became second in command as Caesar after working his way up the Roman government under the Emperor Diocletian.

He was raised in the Emperor Diocletian. He received an outstanding education and learned to write and read in Greek and Latin. In addition, he learned theater, mythology, and Greek philosophy. Even though he was raised in a life of privilege, in different ways he was held hostage by Emperor Diocletian to ensure his father would remain loyal.

V. PRKUSIĆ
Diocletian's Palace

Holy Land, Jerusalem

HIS FAMILY

Constantine directed Helena, his mother, to go to the Holy Land where she was able to discover some remnants of the cross that Jesus had been crucified on. Early in 326 he ordered that Fausta, his wife, and Crispus, his son be put to death.

HIS EARLY CAREER

He served as a part of the Roman army for many years. In addition, he watched Diocletian's murder and persecution of the Christians. Observing this massacre affected him for a long time.

One Diocletian became ill, he proceeded to name Galerius to be his heir. Since Galerius felt that Constantine's father was a rival, this made Constantine fear for his life. Some reports indicate that while Galerius attempted to kill him by different methods, Constantine managed to survive these attempts on his life.

Constantine was eventually able to flee and join his father in Gaul, located in the Western Roman Empire. He proceeded to spend a year fighting along with his father.

Constantius Chlorus

Constantine the Great
Y THIS SIGN CONQUER

BECOMING EMPEROR

Once his father fell ill, Constantine was named Emperor of the Roman Empire's western lands. He then became ruler of Spain, Gaul, and Britain. He then started building up and strengthening much of this area, which including building cities and roadways. His rule then moved to Trier, located in Gault, and proceeded to strengthen this city's power and also built public buildings.

He started conquering the kings around him with his huge army. The portion of this Roman Empire under his rule was expanded. People starting viewing him as a great leader. He was also able to stop the harassment of Christians living in his area.

First church commissioned by Constantine

Maxentius

THE CIVIL WAR

Once Galerius passed away around 311 AD, many of the stronger men decided that they wanted to rule over the Roman Empire and a civil war ensued. Maxentius proceeded to declare himself as Rome's new Emperor. He resided in Rome, then gained control of Italy and Rome. Constantine, along with his army then marched against him.

HE HAS A DREAM

In 312, as he approached Rome, he became increasingly worried. His army was only half of the size of Maxentius' army. Constantine experienced a dream the night before he was to face Maxentius. During this dream, he was advised he could win this battle if he was able to fight under the Christian Cross sign. On the following day, he directed his soldiers to paint a cross on their shields. They proceeded to dominate this battle, and defeated Maxentius, thus taking over control of Rome.

Remains of the Basilica of Maxentius and Constantine

Arch of Constantine

Some reports indicate that during this dream he did not see the cross, but rather saw Chi and Rho, which are Greek letters that represent Christ in the Greek language.

BECOMING A CHRISTIAN

Once he took control of Rome, he then established a coalition in the east with Licinius. During 313, the Edict of Milan was signed, stating that the Roman Empire could no longer persecute the Christians. He now deemed himself as a supporter of the Christian faith.

Battle of Constantine and Licinius

Baptism of Constantine

His closest mentors consisted of bishops such as Lactantius, Hosius, and Eusebius of Caesarea. He selected a group of Christians that had converted to high ranks in this Empire. These Christian ministers had special privileges and he extended several benefits to pagan priests that converted to Christian ministers. One such example would be that they would receive money from the Empire and did not have to pay taxes.

These bishops were faithful as army, but other than the creation of temples, laws and his show of support for this increasing group of priests, he didn't appear much of a Christian. He was in agreement with bishops' recommendations to enact laws against this magic and private divination. However, if no changes occurred in these types of laws by an influential bishop, he had no interest in attempting to make these changes.

Temple of Aphrodite

With Constantine's decree, most of the pagan temples were demolished. For instance, he ordered that the Temple of Aphrodite in London be damaged, as well as several other ceremonial pagan locations. It seemed to be that his interested was in destroying some of the pre-Christian cult locations, however, they were not all to be destroyed.

In each decision to destroy one, it was noted that it couldn't exist as it had been the home of misguided ceremonies and rites, a location of true obstinacy. While he did not ban these rituals outright, he did close and destroyed the more important temples once the bishops decided they were dangerous to their faith.

Saint Constantine & Elena church

Arch of Constantine

Other than Constantine's political motives supporting the growth in the army of priests, he may have had a secret. Even more interesting, it seems that Rome's bishop knew of it, and supported him. The truth became evident that he seemingly supported this newer religion, but still worshipped the Sun and the pagan symbols.

He was raised in the court of the emperor Constantine Chlorus. Emperor Chlorus was a Neoplatonist and was devoted to the Unconquered Sun. Empress Helena, who was his mother, was a Christian travelling the Middle East in search of key locations related to Jesus.

Helena

Ancient texts reveal that she was the person that was able to identify the more important locations known in the Bible. As a youngster, Constantine did not appear to follow the religious interests of his mother. He was known to worship the Sun, a devotee of Mithraism.

In 312, after he was officially converted to Christianity, he built the triumphal arch in Rome. It seems interesting that this arch was not dedicated to Christianity symbols, but rather to the Unconquered Sun. During Constantine's reign, he was able to change several aspects relating to the pagan cults, but this did not mean that he was able to stop the cultivations of the older traditions.

He would give them different names, but would allow for the pagan practices to continue in several ways. In 321, for example, he enacted a law that celebrated the Day of the Sun be a state holiday, which meant a day off for all.

EMPEROR OF ROME

Licinius made a decision seven years later to again begin the persecuting the Christians. Constantine did not like this and then decided to march against Licinius. After many battles, he defeated Licinius and in 324 became the ruler of Rome, which was now united.

Battle between the Fleets of Constantine and Licinius

The Basilica of Constantine and Maxentius

BUILDING ROME

He built several structures, including an enormous basilica located in the forum, leaving his mark on Rome. He also remodeled the Circus Maximus so that it could hold more people. His most notable building might be the Arch of Constantine, which is located in Rome. In addition, he had a massive arch built to memorialize his triumph over Maxentius.

CONSTANTINOPLE

He established the new capital of this Empire in 330 AD. It was built in the ancient city of Byzantium. It was named Constantinople after the Constantine the Emperor and later became the Eastern Roman Empire capitol, also referred to as the Byzantine Empire.

Constantinople

DEATH

Constantine was not baptized as Christian until just prior to passing away. Until he passed away in 337, he ruled this Empire. He was then laid to rest in Constantinople at the Church of the Holy Apostles.

Constantinople was the richest and the largest city until falling to the Ottoman Empire in 1453. It is now known as Istanbul, Turkey's capital.

Constantinople, Turkey

CONSTANTINE BY TH[...]

CHRISTIAN, GOD, OR PAGAN

After he died, he became a pagan god. An examination of the archaeological sites implies that he, similar to other Roman emperors, never ceased to see himself to be son of the ancient deities. It's difficult to believe that his Christian beliefs were strong like those of his mother, Helena. He seems to be more of an intellectual politician than someone that truly desired to Christianize the world.

For additional information about Constantine the Great and Ancient Rome, be sure to research the internet, go to your local library, and ask questions of your teachers, family and friends.

Old Jerusalem

Visit

BABY PROFESSOR
EDUCATION KIDS

www.BabyProfessorBooks.com

to download Free Baby Professor eBooks
and view our catalog of new and exciting
Children's Books